Options Trading for Beginners

A simple Guide to investing and making profit with options trading in Few Weeks

By

Joseph Stone

Contents

Introduction

Options' trading is not for everyone, especially if you lack discipline in your trading. Furthermore, you will not be profitable unless you have a proper setup with an accuracy of at least 80%. Similarly, if you don't have proper money management in place, you'll almost certainly lose money when trading options. Furthermore, if you don't master the art of loss-cutting, you might end up losing a lot of money. Options' trading is not the field for you if you lack patience, can't control your greed, or can't stop averaging your losing position. Furthermore, if you are unable to stop overtrading and use ITM Options, you will be in serious trouble when trading options. On top of all of this, if you can't stop gambling and resist taking BTST and STBT trades, you might end up losing all of your investment. You can always make money trading options if you trade with discipline and have the right setup with an accuracy of at least 80%. Similarly, if you have proper money management in place and are skilled at cutting losses in small increments, you can successfully avoid huge losses in options trading. In options trading, your patience will always be the key to your success. So you don't have to be concerned about trading options if you have the patience to wait for the right opportunity and only trade 2–3 times per day. Furthermore, if you can control your greed and break your bad habit of averaging your position, you will always be able to make money trading options. If you don't overtrade and aren't afraid to use ITM options, you won't have any problems with options trading. If you let go of your gambling attitude and instead start trading with the right mindset and trading strategies, you can easily make money in options trading. You will always be a winner in options trading if you think about keeping your capital first by preventing risky trades like STBT or BTST. The riskiest tool is the option; if the trade goes against you, you could lose a lot of money. A trader's primary goal should be to conserve capital, with profit as a secondary goal. Option trading is worthwhile if it generates profits. You don't trade for the sake of making a few good trades. Similarly, you don't trade to see the green and red numbers on the monitor screen flicker. The value is derived from the outcomes. Without a doubt, if you believe in your trading ability and have faith in your trading strategy, you can become a millionaire through trading options. If you have the ability to maximize your winning trade and have the courage to quit a losing trade, then options trading will be a piece of cake for you. You do not have to be over aggressive, and must learn and practice to trade in your comfort zone while taking positions in options market

CHAPTER 1: What is Options Trading?

An option is a contract that allows (but does not obligate) an investor to buy or sell an underlying instrument such as a security, ETF, or index at a specific price over a specific time period. The options market, that trades contracts based on securities, is where you buy and sell options. A "call option" is one which allows you to buy shares at a later date, whereas a "put option" allows you to sell shares at a later date. Options, on the other hand, are not the same as stocks in that they do not constitute ownership in a company. And, while futures and options both use contracts, options are considered to be less risky because you can withdraw-or walk away from- an options contract at any time. The option's premium (price) is therefore a %age of the underlying asset or security. When a trader or investor buys or sells options, that particular investor or trader has the right to exercise the option at any time up until the expiration date; therefore, simply buying or selling an option does not imply that you must exercise it at the buy/sell point. Options are classified as derivative securities because of this system. This means that options price is derived from something else (in this case, from the value of assets like the market, securities or other basic instruments). As a result, options are frequently regarded as less risky than stocks (if used correctly). Why would an investor, on the other hand, use options? Basically, buying options is betting on stocks to go up, down, or to hedge a market trading position. The "strike price" is the price at which you promise to buy the underlying security via the option, and the "premium" is the fee you pay to purchase that option contract. When deciding on the strike price, you're betting on whether the asset (usually a stock) will rise or fall in value. The premium, which is a percentage of the asset's value, is the price you pay for that bet.

1.1 Options-Past and Present

Modern options contracts were instituted when the Chicago Board of Options Exchange (CBOE) was established, but it is believed that the fundamental concept of options contracts was established in Ancient Greece: possibly as long ago as in the mid-4th century BC. Since then, options have been present in different markets in one form or another, right up until the creation of the CBOE in 1973, when they were appropriately standardized for the first time and trading of options gained some credibility. In scope and sophistication, today's futures markets vary greatly from the barter systems that were first set up by the Japanese. Advances in technology have made trading options and futures more readily available to the average investor, as you might suspect. Most options and futures are electronically executed and pass through the Options Clearing Corporation (OCC), a clearing agency. Their global reach is a new feature of today's futures and options markets. Most big countries have vast markets and exchanges of futures on products ranging from weather, commodities, stocks, and now even returns from Hollywood films. The futures market has global breadth, just like the stock market. It is not without risk to globalize futures exchanges. Fundamentals and psychology of market turned down with significant intensity, as we saw during the meltdowns of last decade, mainly due to derivative protections. The results for the stock and futures markets might have been much worse had there been no government intervention.

What are Options?

Options are securities which grant the investor the option to purchase or sell an asset at a predetermined price, called the strike price, over a specified period of time, without any specific precondition. The amount of time may be as brief as a day, or as lengthy as a few years, depending on the form of contract available. There are only two forms of regular contracts with options: a call and a put. Trading options is simple to understand, as long as you learn certain important points. Investor portfolios are generally built with multiple asset classes. These could include stocks, bonds, ETFs and even mutual funds. Options are another asset class and offer many advantages that trading stocks and ETFs alone cannot possibly offer when used correctly. Like other asset classes, options can be purchased with an investment account. Options are powerful, because they can improve the portfolio of an individual. They do this by adding income, providing protection and even leverage. Depending on the case, there is typically a scenario of options tailored to the target of an investor. To limit downside losses, a popular example would be to use options as an efficient hedge against a falling stock market. Also, options can be used to generate recurring revenues. In addition, they are commonly used for gambling reasons, such as wagering on stock direction. Trading of options involves certain risks which the investor must be aware of before making a trade. Options involve risks and are not appropriate for everyone. Trading of options may be risky in nature and bear significant risk of failure.

- An option is a contract that gives the buyer the right, but not the obligation, to buy or sell (in the case of a call) the underlying asset at a specific price on or before a specific date.

- Traders use income, speculation and risk-hedging options.

- Options are also referred to as derivatives since they derive their value from the underlying assets.

- A stock option contract usually comprises 100 percent of the underlying stock, but options can be drawn up on some type of underlying properties, from debt to currency to product.

1.2 Types of Options

There are two options. It is important to note; the owner is not obliged to exercise his or her right to buy or sell for both types of option contracts. A brief description and roles of each is given below:

1.2.1 Call Option

A call option contract grants the owner the right to purchase 100 shares of a specified security within a specified time frame at a specified price. A call b provides you the right to buy a stock at a certain price on a certain date, with the expiration option. The call buyer will give a sum of money known as a premium for this right that the call seller will get. Not Like stocks that can live in perpetuity, after expiration an option will not exist, ending either worthlessly or with some cost.

Parts of Call Option

The following parts contain the major characteristics of an option:

Strike price

The price at which you will purchase the underlying stock

Premium

The cost of the option, for either the buyer or the seller

Expiration

When the option runs out and is settled

Call Option in action

Each option is considered a contract, and the underlying stock contains 100 securities in each deal. Exchanges quote options in terms of interest per unit, not the overall amount you have to pay to buy the deal. For example, on the exchange, an option might be offered at $0.75. And it would charge (100 shares x 1 contract x $0.75), or $75 to purchase one contract.

If the purchase price is over the strike cost at maturity, the call options are in the bank. The call owner may use the option, setting up cash at the strike cost to buy the stock. Or the owner can actually sell the right to another buyer at its good market price.

A call owner earns profit on less than the difference between the strike price and stock price the when the premium is paid. Suppose, for starters, that a dealer purchased a $0.50 call with a $20 strike price, and that supply is $23. The option valued $3 and the trader made a revenue of $2.50.

If the purchase price at maturity falls below the selling amount, otherwise the call is out of the market and expires useless. The call seller retains the option for any premium collected.

1.2.2 Put Option

A put option contract gives the owner the right to sell within a given time frame 100 shares of a specified security at a specified price. Each contract represents 100 shares, or the stock on which the option is based. Putting options enables traders to magnify downward market changes, transforming a slight price decline into a big benefit for the put buyer.

Components of Put Option

The following components contain the major characteristics of an option:

Strike price

A price at which you will sell the main stock

Premium

The cost of the option, for the buyer or the seller

Expiration

When the option runs out and is resolved

Put Option in action

For that privilege, the put buyer pays the put seller a premium per share. At expiry, if the price of the stock is lower than the price of the strike, the put value grows in money. The interest of the put in this case is proportional to the strike price minus the selling price times 100, as each contract contains 100 securities. Unless the price of the stock is greater than the strike, the put is useless.

1.3 How can you trade Calls and Puts?

Four activities can be performed with options:

- Purchase Calls

- Sell calls

- Buy puts

- Sell puts

Buying stock provides a long position for you. Buying a call option will give you a potentially long position in the underlying stock. Short selling of a stock provides you with a short position. Selling a naked or uncovered call in the underlying stock gives you a potential short position. Buying a put option in the underlying stock gives you a potentially short position. Selling a put option gives you a theoretically long place in the stock underlying it. Those who purchase options are classified as investors and others who offer options are named options writers. Here's the big difference between holders and writers:

There is no requirement for call investors and put investors (buyers) to buy or sell. They are granted the opportunity to exercise their privileges. This reduces the chance of options owners to just paying the premium. However, call writers and put writers (sellers) are obliged to buy or sell if the option expires. This means a seller may need to make good on a purchase or sell pledge. It also means that sellers of options are subject to additional, and in certain situations infinite, threats. It ensures writers will risk a lot more than the quality of premium options.

Options Expiration & Liquidity

Also, options can be categorized according to their duration. Short-term options are options which usually terminate within one year. Long-term options with expirations longer than one year are known as shares where the holder hopes for a jump in price in the long-term. LEAPS are similar to standard solutions, they simply last longer. Also, options can be distinguished when their expiry date falls. Sets of options also expire regularly on a Monday, at month's end, or even hourly. Index and ETF choices also often sell expiries annually.

Options and Speculation

A speculator might think a stock's price will rise on the basis of a fundamental analysis or technical analysis. A speculator may purchase stock or purchase a call on stock option. Speculating with an incentive to call — rather than purchasing the stock directly — is appealing to certain traders because options have leverage. An out-of-the-money call option will pay just a few bucks, or just cents, relative to a $100 stock full price.

Options and Hedging

Hedging with options is intended to reduce risk at reasonable expense. Say you intend to buy inventories of equipment. Yet you do want losses to be minimal. You will reduce the downside exposure by utilizing put options, and reap all the upside in a cost-effective manner. Call options may be used by short sellers to reduce losses if incorrect-particularly during a short squeeze.

1.4 Options Trading and its benefits

Options provide more strategic (and economic) leeway to investors than they can get by just selling, buying, or shorting stocks. Traders can use portfolio loss protection options, snag a security for less than it manages to sell on the open market (or sell it for more), maximize the total returns on an existing or new position, and reduce the risk of speculative betting under all kinds of market conditions. Yes, in the pros vs. cons of options trading, there are a lot of positives. But there are inherent risks as well. Here are some things that should be considered by every prospective options trader.

You do not require large funds to initiate options' trading

An options' purchasing cost (the premium along with the trading commission) is comparatively much lower than what a trader would have to pay to buy securities directly. Traders pay less money to play in the same sandbox, but they will gain just as much (percentage-wise) if the trade goes their way.

Options are comparatively less risky as compared to other trading instruments

You are not required to follow through on the trade when you purchase a put or call option. If your assumptions are incorrect about the time frame and direction of the trajectory of a stock, your losses are limited to anything you paid for the contract as well as trading fees.

You are free to opt for different trading strategies

Before the expiry of an options contract, investors have the liberty to use various strategic moves, including:

- Use the option and purchase the shares to add to their portfolio

- Use the option, purchase the shares and then sell some or all of them

- Sell the "in the money" options contract to a different investor

- Has the option to recover some of the money incurred on an "out of the money" option. This can be done by selling the contract to another investor before its expiry

Options offer the trader to choose price

Option contracts allow investors to freeze the stock price at a specific amount of dollars (the strike price) for a specific period of time. Based on the type of option used, it ensures that investors will be able to purchase the stock at the strike price any time before the expiry of option contract.

1.5 Basics of Options' Pricing

The value of stock options is determined from their underlying shares' value and, depending on the results of the associated shares, the trading price for options can increase or decrease. With options, there are a variety of elements to understand.

The Strike Price

The strike price for an option is the rate at which, if the option is exercised, the underlying asset is purchased or sold. In the peculiar jargon of options, the relationship between the strike price and a stock's market price determines the following:

- Option is in-the-money

- Options is at-the-money

- Option is out-of-the-money

In-the-money

The strike price of an in-the-money call option is below the real market price. Example: At the $95 strike price for WXYZ, an investor buys a call option that is already trading at $100. The investor's position is $5 in-the-money. The call option grants the investor the right to purchase the shares at $95. The strike price of an In-the-Money Put option is above the real market price. Example: At the WXYZ's $110 strike price, which is currently trading at $100, an investor buys a Put option. In-the-money is $10 for this investor position. The Put option grants the seller the right to sell equity at $110.

At the money

For both Put and Call options, the strike and the actual stock prices are the same.

Out-of-the-money

The strike price of an out-of-the-money call option is above the real market price. Example: At the strike price of $120 for ABCD, which is actually trading at $105, an investor buys an out-of-the-money call option. The position of this investor is $15 out-of-the-money. The strike price of an out-of-the-money put option is below the real market price. Example: At the $90 strike price of ABCD, which is currently priced at $105, an investor buys an out-of-the-money Put option. The position of that investor is $15 out-of-the- money.

The Premium

The premium is the price for an option that a customer pays to the seller. On purchasing, the premium is paid up front and is not reimbursable- even though the option is not applied. Premiums on a per-share basis are quoted. So, a $0.21 premium reflects a $21.00 per option contract ($0.21 x 100 shares) premium payment. There are many considerations that decide the amount of the premium-the prevailing stock price in comparison to the strike price (intrinsic value), the period of time before the offer expires (time value) and the price fluctuations of the commodity (volatility value).

Intrinsic value + Value of time + Value of volatility = option price

For example, at a strike price of $80, an investor buys a three-month call option for a volatile security that trades at $90.

Intrinsic Value = $10

Time value = because the call is 90 days away, the time value will be slightly applied to the price.

Volatility value = Because the underlying security is volatile, the volatility premium might be added.

Factors impacting options prices

Following factors have an impact on options prices:

- The underlying equity price in relation to the strike price (intrinsic value)

- The length of time until the option expires (time value)

- How much the price fluctuates (volatility value)

Additional factors that have an impact on option prices

Additional facts that have an impact on options prices are:

- The underlying equity's quality

- The underlying equity's dividend rate

- Prevailing market conditions

- The underlying equity's supply and demand for options

- The existing interest rates

Additional costs: Taxes and commissions

Investors that trade options, as in virtually any investment, must pay income taxes and also commissions to brokers on options trades. The net profit gain would be impacted by these costs.

1.6 Pricing Spreads in Options and Trading Strategies

A call spread relates to the purchasing of a call on a strike, and the selling of another call for a higher strike of the same expiry. An option strategy in which a call option is purchased is a call spread, and another less costly call option is sold. A put spread relates to purchasing a put on a strike, and selling another put on the same expiry's lower price. An option technique in which a put option is purchased is a put spread, and another less costly put option is sold. This transaction is less dangerous than an outright buy, since the call and put options have identical features, but it often provides less benefit. If you think that the underlying price will shift in a certain direction, and wish to reduce your original outlay if the forecast is wrong, these techniques are beneficial to try.

Advantages of Spreads

When you want to mitigate risk, spreads are useful for trading. Typically, spreads are traded by arbitragers to gain an edge on the transaction with close strikes, and then control the position. Position takes in trading premiums as the short option premium tends to cover the cost of the long option.

Call spreads buying considerations

Consider buying call spreads in the following situations:

- If you are sure that the underlying security is destined to go up after which volatility will subside(e.g. a news event)
- When you are sure that the underlying security is definitely going to edge up moderately
- When you are sure that the underlying security's price will decline sharply, thus generating a sale of the underlying security
- Consequently, the call spread will guard you against a petty upside move

Put spreads buying considerations

Consider buying put spreads in the following situations:

- If you are sure that the underlying security is going to edge downward resulting in decrease in volatility (e.g. a news event)

- If you are sure that the underlying security is going to depict decline in a limited range

- If you are sure that the underlying security is going to fall sharply

Bull call spread

One long call along with a lower strike price plus one short call at a higher strike price is a bull call spread. The very underlying stock and the same expiry period are required for both calls. For a net debit (or net cost) and gains as the underlying stock increases in price, a bull call spread is built. Profit is impaired if the stock price increases above the short call strike price, and the possible loss is restricted if the stock price moves below the long call strike price (lower risk).

Bear Call Spread

A bear call spread, or a bear call credit spread, is a form of strategy of options which is used when an options trader believes the cost of the main stock to fall. By buying call options at a particular strike price although selling the same amount of calls at the same maturity date, but at a low strike cost, a bear call spread is established. Using this technique, the full profit to be made is equivalent to the credit earned while beginning the trade.

A short call spread is another name for a bear call spread. It is deemed as a strategy with limited-risk and limited-reward.

Calendar call spreads

You sell and purchase a call with the same strike price while running a calendar spread with calls, but the call you purchase would have a later date of expiry than the call you sell. As expiration approaches, you take advantage of accelerating time decay on the front-month call, also known as shorter-term call. You want to purchase back the shorter-term call right before the front-month expiration for almost nothing. You will sell the back-month call and close your position at the same moment. Ideally, there would also be considerable time value for the back-month call.

Bear Put Spread

A bear put spread consists of a higher strike price for one long put and a lower strike price for one short put. Both puts have the same underlying stock and the same expiry date. For a net debit (or net cost) and earnings as the underlying stock decreases in price, a bear put spread is created. Profit is restricted if the stock price falls below the lower strike price of the short put strike), and if the stock price increases above the long put strike price (higher strike), the possible loss is limited.

Bull Put spread

A bull put spread consists of a higher strike price for a short put and a lower strike price for a long put. Both puts have the same underlying security and the same expiry date. For a net credit (or net sum received) and gains from either an increasing equity price or from time erosion or from both, a bull put spread is created. Potential benefit is restricted to the net premium earned less commissions and potential loss is reduced if the stock price drops below the long put strike price.

Calendar put spread

By purchasing one "longer-term" put and selling one "shorter-term" put with the similar strike cost, a long calendar spread with puts is established. Consider the following example. 100 Put is bought for two months (56 days to expiration) and 100 Put is sold for one month (28 days to expiration). For a net debit (net cost), this strategy is established and both the profit opportunity and the risk are minimal. If the stock price matches the strike price of the puts on the closing date of the short put, the maximum profit is obtained and the maximum risk is achieved if the stock price shifts sharply away from the strike price.

CHAPTER 2: Fundamentals of Options Trading

To better understand options trading, let's look at a simple example. Assume you're purchasing a stock for US$ 300. However, the broker informs you of an exciting offer: you can buy it now for US$ 300 or give a token amount of US$ 30 and reserve the right to buy it at US$ 300 in a month's time, even if the stock's value rises during that time. However, that small sum is non-refundable. You recognize that the stock has a good chance of crossing US$ 330, and thus you can at least break even. Because you only have to pay US$ 30 now, you can put the rest of the money towards something else for a month. You wait a month before checking the stock price. You now have the option of buying the stock from the broker or not, depending on the stock price. Of course, this is an oversimplification, but this is the essence of options trading. Options are derivatives, which means their price is derived from elsewhere, most commonly stocks, in the world of trading. An option's price is inextricably linked to the underlying stock's price.

2.1 How to buy a Call Option?

When the cost of the underlying asset rises to a price better than the strike price of the contract, the buyer of the option call seeks to benefit. The call option seller, on the other hand, expects the asset's price to fall, or at the very least never increase as high as the exercise price / strike value, before the option expires, in case the money taken for selling the option will be genuine incomprehensible profit. For example, imagine you've purchased an option on 100 stocks, with a $30 option to hit. Before your option runs out, the stock price increases from $28 to $40. You will then exercise the right to purchase 100 stock options at $30, granting you an instant $10 a share benefit. Your overall income will be 100 options, $10 for a share, minus the sales price you were charged for the option. If you had paid 200 dollars for the call option in this case, then your total income will be 800 dollars (100 shares x $10/share-$ 200 equals to $800).

Buying call options helps buyers to spend a small sum of money to theoretically profit from the rate increase in the underlying security, or to guard from the positional risks.

2.2 How to sell a Call Option?

Sellers of call options, also called writers, offer call options in the expectation that they may become useless by the expiry date. They earn money by pocketing the rates (prices) they have been paying. An income would be decreased, or possibly turn into a total loss, if the option holder performs the option profitably as the underlying security cost falls past the option strike point. The call options are offered in two ways:

Covered Call Option

If the call option seller holds the underlying stock, then a call option is covered. To Sell the call options on the underlying securities brings in extra gain, which would mitigate any anticipated market price decreases. The seller option is "covered" compared to a loss since if the buyer option exercises its option, the seller can provide the buyer with stock shares which he has already bought at a low price than the option's strike price. The seller's income in holding the underlying stock would be restricted to raising the stock to the strike price, but he will be shielded from any real loss.

Naked Call Option

A naked call option is one that is sold by an option seller who does not own the underlying stock. Because there is no limit on how higher the price of a stock can go and the owner of the option is not "protected" by holding the underlying stock against future losses, naked short selling of options is regarded exceedingly dangerous. When a call option holder practices his or her right, the bare option seller is compelled to buy the shares at the current market price and deliver the securities to the option holder. The gap between the current market price and the strike price reflects the seller's loss if the stock price surpasses the strike price of the call option. To compensate for any potential losses, most option sellers charge the full cost.

2.3 How to buy and sell a Put Option?

You can produce double-digit salary and returns by selling put options even in a bearish, flat, or overvalued market. For big returns on investment, you do not require a great bull market or rapid business growth. In the case of a market collapse, you may even grant your investments 10 per cent guarantee against downside. In other words, if the market falls by 25%, your equity positions are likely to fall by only 15%. You can also enter stock positions exactly at the price you want and keep the cost base low. You should try to purchase in a declining market to get a greater bargain instead of buying at presently available market rates. Like any device, there is a perfect period and place for selling put options and certain times it is not an optimal strategy. This is a sophisticated and best way of entering equity positions, when used correctly. To option sellers, the two most critical things are the bid and the strike. The strike is the price on which you agree to purchase the shares for if the option is used, and the bid is about the amount you can presume to earn on selling the option. If you sell an option with a strike price of 30 dollars less than the current stock price of 30.50 dollars, you will now receive $143 from the option buyer, and you will be obliged to purchase 100 shares of the company at $30 each if the buyer wishes, for an over-all of $3,000, at any time before the option expires in 3½ months. If the particular company's stock generally stays above $30 / share over the next 3½ months, the option buyer probably won't assign the shares to you, as When the market rate is already above $30 a share, there's no need for her to compel you to pay absolutely $30 a share. Her option will end worthlessly, you will keep your $143 premium, and your $3,000 in protected cash will be released for another option to be sold. Here is the calculated rate of return, if the right expires: $143 / $2,857 = 0.05 = 5%

After around 3.5 months, you made a return yield of 5 per cent on your early currency. This will be around 18 percent annual returns on your investment if you practice that for the remainder of the year a few of times. Compare this with the historical return of S&P 500 of around 9%. Compared to average stock returns, you're being charged a huge amount of money to only hang around and wait on for a market drop on a business you'd like to buy. On the contrary, if the stock dips to $29.50 per share, you still have to retain the 143 dollars premium, and the buyer option will appoint you to purchase the 100 shares for 30 dollars each. It means that your effective price base for buying those shares was just $28.57, which, as you wanted, is less than your target buy cost. You ended up purchasing them for $30 apiece, but you still got a $1.43 / share bonus up front, which covered some of the expense. The total cost structure is that for 100 securities you have to spend $28.57 / share, or $2.857. So instead, you hold 100 shares of a company already selling for $29.50 each. You purchased a wonderful business at a decent price and ideally you should still anticipate lots of growth in profits and bonuses over time.

CHAPTER 3: Getting Started in Option Trading

Options trading was once thought to be a practice that was best for financial professionals, but it has grown in popularity among individual investors over time. Options trading reached a daily average of more than twenty million contracts per day in 2018, a new high compared to previous years. Trading options can benefit new and beginning investors, and they can use measures to guard against risk as well as increase their profit potential. Trading options can add a lot of flexibility to your investment strategy when you consider volatility, time value and interest rates. You'll have to learn the language before you begin. Understanding what a strike price is and the difference between call and put options is crucial to fully comprehending what you're getting yourself into. You'll need a trading account with an options brokerage to begin trading options. After you've set up the account, you could start trading options with your broker, who will execute the trades for you. We have explained the basic concepts in the previous chapters. It's relatively easy to get started with options trading, despite the fact that it might sound complex and can include a wide range of strategic approaches. You'll need a broker, and you should compare fees as well as account minimums to find one that fits your budget and investment style. Then it's time to come up with an options trading strategy. Options trading strategies, like most investments, are dependent on your specific objectives and risk profile, and can range from simple to complex. It is time to acquaint yourself with certain prerequisites for options trading.

3.1 Open a Trading Account

You will be asked if you want to open a cash account or a margin account when you open a trading account with a brokerage firm.

Cash Account vs. Margin Account

The difference between a margin account and a cash account is that a margin account enables you to borrow funds from the brokerage by using your existing holdings (such as stocks and/or long-term options) as collateral. You can only use the cash in the account to pay for all of your stock and option trades if you have a cash account.

Minimum Deposit

A minimum deposit is usually required for opening a trading account. The amount required varies according to the type of account you're opening and the brokerage firm. To open a cash account, you only need a small deposit, whereas federal regulations demand a minimum deposit of $2000 for opening a margin-enabled account.

Online Brokerage vs. Offline Brokerage

Trading options effectively requires using an online brokerage account because there are lots of variables in an options trade compared to a stock trade. When you have to communicate too many details about a trade to the broker over the phone, you run the risk of miscommunication, which can be very costly. With today's advanced technology, online brokerages for options now provide highly intuitive user interfaces that make placing option trades online far easier than doing so over the phone. Furthermore, whilst a human broker can only deal with one client at a time, online brokerages can deal with thousands of orders at the same time. As a result, it's no matter of chance that the rise of option trading parallels the phenomenal advancement of internet technologies.

3.2 Things To Know As A Beginner

If you're thinking about trading options for generating profits, you may wonder if it's a decent time to start trading. Guidelines are available that you could always follow.

Be aware of minimum account required for trading options

To trade options, each online broker needs a different minimum

balance. The mandatory minimum deposit for most brokerages is less than $1,000. Investors fill out a brief questionnaire inside their investment account to submit for options trading authorization. It is possible to get access to begin executing options directly afterwards.

Clear all debt

Get out of debt first. Pay off the car loans and credit card balances, explicitly. It's because of those loans, you're losing income anyway. Instances of' good debt' are known to be leases and student loans, while auto loans and credit card balances are perceived as instances of' bad debt.' The bottom line is that, before you start trading options, you must get out of bad debt.

Don't get stressed out while learning to trade options

You're also not fully in a spot to trade options even after you've eliminated the bad debt. You first have to know yourself. And if you believe you're ready and in the past you traded stocks, you still aren't done. Trading options are totally separate from trading securities. And before you trade options, you have to understand the stock market. However, you still need to learn quite a bit more. Start by studying the essentials. Understand the distinction between options for call and options for put. Know about expiration dates for contracts and strike prices. The trading of options is for persons who delve extensively into the data to assess the most advantageous trades. Traders who overlook certain stats are sometimes burnt.

Learning is the key to success

When it applies to options trading, you have never "arrived." There is always something that an expert trader will learn from you. Keep practicing also though you have trained yourself and mastered trading to the extent that you value your expertise as a trader. Strive to make yourself a greater trader every day.

Keep practicing

Before you allocate real capital, you need to do some practice trading. This is because, before doing the real thing, everybody wants to do some practice trading. When you invest in the capital markets, there are things you can learn. The quick way rather than the rough way is easier to learn such lessons. Fortunately, trading platforms are accessible that enable you to learn trading. Without losing some of your hard-earned assets, you can establish a pretend portfolio and begin trading stocks and options. And, as time progresses, you will see how the trades are successful. Take the time to assess what went wrong if you're not profitable, so that you can stop making such errors in the future.

Be aware of prerequisites for opening an Options trading account

Stock market options are limited-term contracts that offer owners the right to purchase or sell particular securities at a fixed date. In a broad variety of market techniques, the two forms of options — puts and calls — may be used to benefit from potential shifts in equity prices. To start purchasing and selling puts and calls, you must first register for account authorization. A trading account for options is a cash, margin or IRA stock brokerage account to which trading authorization for options has been applied. By completing a separate document, you incorporate options permission, plus a declaration of your trading background. The regulatory department of the broker checks the application for options and accepts your account with a degree of trading permission varying from one to five. What options strategies may be traded in the account are decided by the authorization levels. Novice investors can obtain one or two levels of authorization that enable strategies for lower-risk options.

You should be able to read a contract

Option contracts are purchased and sold using the online investment account's options trading screen. Under the options-chain link of a given stock, various put and call option choices can be identified. Choosing an option from the chain fills the trading screen with the specifics of a single option. You may then decide how many contracts you choose to purchase or sell and, if necessary, set a cap price. For a market order, the currently quoted "bid" price of an option is what you will pay to purchase. If you sell on the market, the "bid" price is what you would get. Each option contract is on an underlying stock of 100 securities, so one contract costs 100 times the quoted amount.

Should have sound knowledge of open and close orders

To start a trading position, options may be either bought or sold. Buying options grants you the right to purchase (call options) and/or sell (put options) the actual stock securities at a particular amount. If the customer uses his privileges under the options you have sold, trading options adds option premium earnings to the portfolio and the obligation to sell or purchase stock. You execute a buy-to-open or sell-to-open order to open an options position, depending on your approach. The order would be a sell-to-close or buy-to-close to close an options position in your portfolio.

Must have knowledge of Options Trading Platforms

To an online broker, there is no consumer more important than an options investor. Trades of options give brokers far larger operating profits than equity trades, and competitiveness is fierce for attracting these consumers as a consequence. This sort of business environment is perfect for consumers because product creativity and efficient prices come with fair competition. One can check for the following important characteristics when choosing a trading platform:

- Speed

- Low costs

- Options tools

The desktop application should have easy trading and intensive analysis. Option software should have personalized classification, real-time Greek streaming, and specialized position analysis for existing positions. It must give and show all the resources that an options trader would like in an efficient way. Some of them could be spread groupings, easy strategy screening, and risk / reward details that are simple to grasp. It must encourage customers to build custom rules and instantly roll up their current options positions. It should be outstanding for the amount of settings and depth of choice. Trading platforms can be built for both novice and experienced options traders. You as an investor should expect from your broker to include scanning, P&L analysis, risk analysis, and easy-order management.

The Broker's selection

Trading profitably allows you to use a brokerage company that aligns with your financial priorities, educational requirements and personal style. Choosing the right online stock broker that suits your needs, particularly for new investors, may mean the difference between an exciting new income stream and crushing disappointment.

Margins

In options dealing, "margin" often applies to the cash or assets needed to be deposited with the brokerage company by an option writer as collateral for the obligation of the writer to purchase or sell the underlying security or, in the case of cash-settled options, to compensate the balance of the cash payout if the option is assigned.

Margin call

In the case of an unfavorable market movement, margins are needed to guarantee that you will fulfill your future obligations. Margins are payable for option writers only, while buyers of options do not.

An Options margin call is where the broker needs extra cash or stocks to be given by a customer who has written Options. A failure to fulfill a margin call can result in closing of your Options positions.

How are Margins triggered

A margin call can be triggered for a score of factors, but the most common reasons are:

- When a position moves against you, it consequently increases your potential obligation under the Options contract.

- The exchange increases the margin requirement against your positions. The exchange reduces the collateral value allowed on your shares deposited as cover.

CHAPTER 4: Step-By-Step Guide To Gain From Options

It is time that you learn in a sequential manner about options' trading style and steps required to make money with options.

4.1 First Step: Find the correct setups

To begin, you must first identify an underlying asset on which to trade options. You shouldn't just pick any asset here. You should search for specific criteria and trade options that meet all of them. Following are the important factors to consider when selecting assets for options trading.

Liquidity

When trading options, liquidity is perhaps the most essential factor to consider. Liquidity refers to how easy or difficult it is to exit and enter positions in each asset. High liquid assets are those that have a large volume, tough Bid/Ask spreads, and are thus simple to exit and enter. If you prefer to trade an illiquid asset, you may have difficulty exiting and entering positions, and there is a risk of losing money. As a result, it's critical to concentrate on assets that are extremely liquid and have a high volume. You should consider more than just the underlying asset's liquidity. You should also consider the liquidity of the underlying asset's options. It can be achieved by looking at some options' volume, Bid/Ask prices, and open interest. In general, you should switch to indices, ETFs, and stocks that are heavily traded and well-known. Most of these renowned assets must be liquid, with liquid options. Simply avoid an asset that isn't liquid enough.

Implied Volatility (IV)

The implied volatility of an underlying asset is the next important factor to consider when choosing one to trade. The impact of implied volatility on option pricing can be significant. As a result, knowing whether IV is high or low is critical. IV Rank can be used to determine whether IV is currently high or low. It's crucial to choose assets with high-level implicit volatility when selling options. As a result, options will be more expensive, resulting in a higher premium for you as an option seller. When you are selling options, look for liquid assets with an IV Level of at least 50.

The Price

You may not trade options on all the assets depending on the size of your account. If an asset has a lot of costly options and your current account is insignificant, you should probably look for something else. However, different strategies can be used to modify your risk. Some assets have a limited number of options, which can be costly. So, look for an asset that has options that are appropriate for your account size.

Upcoming News / Events

In addition to the previously mentioned facets, you should keep an eye on the asset's upcoming events or news. This can help put the previous points into context. For instance, if a stock has future earnings, indicated volatility will almost certainly be high, as many stocks move significantly after earnings. Prevent assets with major upcoming events, such as earnings. These assets will most likely shift more than new assets, lowering your chances of profit. Also, stay away from assets with a future ex-dividend date, as this can have a significant impact on your chance of assignment and the price of the option.

4.2 Second step: Form a directional assumption

The underlying asset's directional assumption is formed in the second step. Is it more likely to go up, down, or sideward? This step will have an impact on the strategy you choose for the next step. You could use fundamentals or technical analysis to come up with a directional assumption. But to be honest, it doesn't really matter because we're trading with a maximum probability of success. It means that the price of the underlying asset could go against you, but you wouldn't lose money right away. You should be able to profit if the underlying asset does not move dramatically. Few (high probability option) traders believe that agreeing on a direction is continually a 50/50 bet. As a result, many traders prefer to trade neutral strategies rather than directional ones. Your directional assumption may be inspired by your present portfolio in the future. You shouldn't do a lot of technical analysis in this situation.

Simply choose whether you're bullish, bearish, or neutral on the underlying asset.

4.3 Third Step: Select a strategy

Finally, it's time to choose a trading strategy. Some of the preceding factors, such as the directional price, assumption, and accessibility of options, should influence this decision. Stocks are less versatile than options. Depending on your directional assumption, you would sell or purchase a stock in stock trading. Options trading, on the other hand, allow you to choose from and merge hundreds of various methods. However, for this trading style, you must concentrate solely on a limited option policy. Because you want to sell options rather than buy them, all these strategies will be generally short approaches. You can pick between defined or undefined probability strategies based on your risk profile. Only certain option trading strategies work with high probability option selling. There are a few key elements that make strategies successful for this style.

Overall Short

You should concentrate on trading overall quick strategies since you will be selling options.

Collecting Premium

Because you are selling something, you should collect a credit to start an overall quick option strategy.

Time Decay

A high-probability option seller, time should be on your side. To put it another way, when opening a new position, the option Greek Theta must be positive. This will enable you to profit from the passage of time.

Implied Volatility

To profit from a drop in implied volatility, the option Greek Vega must be negative. This is a critical point.

High Probability

When selling options, you should have a high chance of profit. Concentrate on setups with a high probability. Don't be too directional, and instead bet on large jumps in any other direction.

4.4 Fourth Step: Find the right option

After you've decided on a strategy, you'll need to decide on an expiry date, strike prices, and other details. This, too, is dependent on individual factors such as account size, risk tolerance, and time. However, as a rule, 45 days before expiration is a better time frame. According to research, the best way to profit from rising time decay is to wait 45 days before it expires. However, you won't always be able to start a position with a 45-day expiration date. It's best to stick to monthly expiration dates and avoid weekly options. Liquidity is the major excuse for this. Weekly options have a lot less open interest and volume than monthly options. When trading options, it's critical to keep your stakes low. Even with a high-powered option trading strategy, you won't always win. There will always be losing trades, and it is critical to keep them small. The only way to achieve this is to deal small amounts on each trade. Never put too much of your account's money into a single trade. It is strongly advised that you keep your chance to a maximum of 1-10 percent of your account per position.

4.5 Fifth Step: Choose the correct price

There is one final thing to ponder before sending out the order, and it is the price. Always make sure you have sufficient balance to establish the trade worthwhile. You must also consider commissions if you have an insufficient amount. The trade is probably not worth if you just get $20 in premium and must pay 7 dollars in commissions. At least $50 must be brought in. You must also consider your reward / risk ratio. Because of the high likelihood of profit, this may not be the good option. Frequently, your maximum risk outweighs your maximum reward. But that's fine if your chances aren't too slim. For instance, you should not risk $1000 in order to get $100 with a 40% chance of profit. Though, take the risk of $250 in order to get $100 with a 75% return is perfectly acceptable. Furthermore, limit orders should always be used. This will result in good pricing and a higher perceived value. Your order can be filled quicker but at a lower price if you use a market order. You can set your own price when you use limit orders. You can frequently get filled at a medium price in highly liquid assets. If you do this, every trade will get you a few dollars. If you add up to hundreds or thousands of dollars, this can be a significant sum of money.

4.6 Sixth Step: Make money with options

You've now completed the trade. This step primarily entails expecting for the sold option(s) to reduce their cost so that you can repurchase them for a lower price than you originally paid. It is suggested that profits be taken at 50% of the maximum profit. This will rise your profit potential while also reducing the time spent on each trade. Getting profits soon will let you to place new trades more rapidly. You could computerize this process by placing a Good Till Cancel (GTC) order at 50% of your maximum profit just after you open your positions. Here's an example of what this could look like:

You get a $1.5 credit for filling a position (as a standard option contract operates 100 shares of stock). You can then continue by sending a $0.75 GTC debit order. The GTC order should be filled as soon as the position drops to around $0.75, and you will be automatically exited.

There are a few management options available if a situation doesn't work out as scheduled. Again, the management options are determined by the strategy you select. Because your risk isn't capped, undefined risk strategies should be handled more than defined risk strategies. Cutting losses at a certain point is a way to control the risk of undefined risk strategies. Another option is to apply the strategy to a credit with a later expiration phase. This can be repeated many times. Because you have a limited downside, handling defined risk strategies isn't as important. This maximum loss should be acceptable if you maintained your position size small enough. There are, however, a few approaches to adjusting defined risk strategies. It's critical not to abandon losing positions too quickly. This may appear to be unrealistic, but it isn't. It is always possible to turn a losing position into a successful one. It will be a guaranteed loss if you get it off at a loss. So, if the loss isn't too large and there's still time before the expiration date, you must try to grip on to losing trades. One more reason why small position sizes are essential is because of this. You will miss out on many potential winners if you must cut losses as soon as a position goes against you. Before the expiration date, several winning option positions are red. You shouldn't, however, keep to obvious losing positions. If you only have a short amount of time left or if a position is going against you then you must take the loss. Losing positions, especially those with less time left, must be rolled out or cleared. Due to assignment risk, this is the case. The risk of being assigned is known as assignment risk. Assignments are made only to short ITM option holders in the final week before expiration. Even with two days to go, a far ITM option isn't assured to be assigned.

4.7 Seventh Step: Start all over again

This is, without a doubt, one of the most crucial steps. If you want to make money with options, you must repeat the similar procedure repeatedly. We'll use an example to demonstrate why it's important to repeat this process:

A coin tossing game is used as an example. The game's rules are in which you toss a coin and if it come heads, you get $1; if it come tails, you lose $1. It's a 50/50 chance. You will be 1 dollar up or 1 dollar down if you toss the coin once. You must have gained 5 times, lost five times or anything in between if you tossed the coin five times. If you tossed the coin ten times, the result would be similar. However, if you toss the coin thousand times, you will almost certainly be at or near breakeven.

We can apply the same concept to our trading. The genuine outcome may differ from the probable outcome if we place 1, 2, or more small trades with a 70% chance of profit. Even if 2 trades have a 70% chance of profiting, they could very well end up being failures. However, if we place 200 trades with a 70% chance of profiting, it is highly not likely that all of them will lose. The more trades we make, the closer we move to our desired result. It is critical that you comprehend this. As a result, it's critical to boost the number of events as much as possible. This does not imply that you should place many trades at the same time. It simply suggests that you must approach this strategy with a long-term mindset. The numbers will eventually work themselves out. All you have to do now is stick with it long enough.

CHAPTER 5: Beginners Common Mistakes

When trading options, you can profit whether the stock price goes up or down or sideways. With a small cash outlay, you could use option strategies to minimize losses, preserve gains as well as handle large portions of stock. When trading options, you could also lose more than the full amount you spent in a small amount of time. That's why it's crucial to proceed cautiously. Even the most experienced traders can make a mistake and lose money. Beginners frequently make the following mistakes.

Buying Out-of-the-Money (OTM) Call Options

One of the most difficult ways to make consistent money in option trading is to buy OTM calls outright. Because they are inexpensive, OTM call options appeal to new option traders. Buying a cheap call option and seeing if you can pick a winner seems like a good place to start. Buying calls may appear safe because it follows the same pattern as buying low and selling high as an equity trader. However, if you only use this strategy, you risk losing money on a regular basis.

Misunderstanding of leverage

Most beginners take advantage of the leverage factor that option contracts provide, unaware of the risk they are taking. They are frequently attracted to buying short-term calls. For new option traders, a general rule is to start with one option if you normally trade 100 share lots. If you usually trade 300 share lots, you might be able to get three contracts. This is a good starting point for a test amount. If you don't succeed in these sizes, you're unlikely to succeed in larger trades.

Absence of exit plan

It's probably something you've heard a thousand times before. It's critical to keep your emotions in check while trading options, just as it is when trading stocks. This does not imply that you must swallow your fears in a superhuman manner. It's much easier than that: make a work schedule and adhere to it. Even when things seem to be going well, you should have a backup plan. Choose an upside and a downside exit point, as well as the timeframes for each exit, well ahead of time. What if you leave some upside on the table by leaving too soon? This is a common trader's concern. The best counter-argument is this: What if you could consistently make a profit, reduce your losses, and get a better night's sleep? Make a plan for how you'll get out of this situation. An exit strategy is essential whether you're buying or selling options. It assists you in developing more successful trading patterns. It also helps you to keep your worries in check. Ascertain an upside exit strategy and a worst-case scenario on the downside that you are willing to accept. Liquidate your position and take the profits if you achieve your upside targets. If you hit your downside stop-loss, you should exit the trade once again. Don't put yourself in any more danger by betting that the option price will rise. The temptation to go against this advice will almost certainly be strong at times. It's not a good idea. You must devise a strategy and then stick to it. Far too many traders devise a strategy and then abandon it as soon as the trade is executed in able to pursue their emotions.

Failure to adopt new strategies

Many option traders claim they would never buy or sell out-of-the-money or in-the-money options respectively. These absolutes seem ridiculous until you're in the middle of a losing trade. Keep an open mind when it comes to developing new option trading strategies. Remember that options are derivatives. This means that their prices do not move in the same way as the underlying stock or even have the same properties. Time decay, whether beneficial or detrimental to the position, must always be incorporated into your plans. You have to decide to close the trade, reduce your losses or look for a new opportunity that makes more sense right now. Options can provide a lot of leverage for a small amount of money, but they can also blow up just as swiftly as any other position if you dig too deep. Accept a small loss in exchange for a chance to avoid a disaster later.

Trading Options that are not liquid

Liquidity refers to a trader's ability to buy or sell something quickly without causing a significant price change. A liquid market is one where buyers and sellers are always ready to buy and sell. Another way to look at it is as follows: The likelihood that the forthcoming trade would be executed at the same price as the previous one is referred to as liquidity. For a simple reason, stock markets are much more liquid than option markets. Option traders might just have dozens of option contracts to choose from, whereas stock traders may only trade one stock. If the stock is extremely illiquid, the options on it are likely to be even less active. The bid as well as ask price for the options will usually have a large spread as a result of this. Trading illiquid options raises the cost of doing business, which is already higher than stock trading costs on a percentage basis. Don't put too much pressure on yourself. Make sure the open interest is at least 40 times the number of contacts you want to trade if you're trading options.

Waiting too long to buy back short options

Traders frequently wait far too long to buy back the options they've sold. There are also plenty of reasons for this. Consider the following scenario:

- You are adamant about not paying the commission.

- You're betting that the contract will be worthless when it expires.

- You want to squeeze out a little more profit from the trade.

Recognize when it's time to repurchase your short options. If the short option becomes far out of the money and you can profitably buy it back, do so. Don't be a miser. Here's a good rule of thumb: if you could somehow keep 80% or more of the profit from the option sale, you should consider buying it back. Otherwise, it's a foregone conclusion. Because you waited too long, a short option will bite you one of these days.

Failure to factor in upcoming events

Although not all market events can be predicted, there are two key activities to keep track of whilst trading options. For example, if you've sold calls and a dividend is approaching, your chances of being assigned early are higher if the option is already in the money. This is particularly true if a sizable dividend is expected. Because option holders do not have a right to a dividend, this is the case. The option trader must exercise the option as well as purchase the underlying stock in order to collect. Make sure to take into account upcoming events. You must, for example, be aware of the ex-dividend date. Also, unless you're willing to take a higher risk of assignment, avoid selling options contracts with pending dividends. Investing during earnings season usually means dealing with higher volatility in the underlying stock – and paying a premium for the option. If you want to buy an option during earnings season, you can create a spread by buying one option and selling another.

Legging into Spreads

Most novice options traders attempt to "leg into" a spread by purchasing one option first and then selling the other. They're attempting to reduce the price by a few pennies. It simply isn't worth taking the chance. If you'd like to trade a spread, don't "leg in." Spreads can be traded as a single trade. Don't take on unnecessary market risk. Always treat a spread as if it were a single trade. Don't get caught up in the details of timing. You want to enter the trade as soon as the market begins to fall.

Not knowing what to do when assigned

If you sell options, just keep in mind that you could be assigned before the expiration date if you sell them early. Many new option traders do not consider assignment as a probability until it occurs to them. Early assignment is one of those irrational and highly emotional market events. When it happens, it usually has no rhyme or reason. It's unavoidable. Even when the market indicates that it is a less-than-successful strategy. Plan ahead of time what you'll do if you're given a task. The best way to avoid an early assignment is to think about it ahead of time. Otherwise, it may lead to rash, spur-of-the-moment decisions that are less than rational.

Ignoring index options for neutral trades

Individual stocks have a high degree of volatility. For example, if a company experiences a major unanticipated news event, the stock may remain extremely bearish for a few days. Even significant turmoil in a major company that is part of the S&P 500, on the other hand, is unlikely to cause the index to fluctuate significantly. Index-based trading options can protect you from the massive swings that single news items can cause in individual stocks. Consider neutral trades on major indices to reduce the unpredictability of market news. Consider trading strategies such as short spreads (also known as credit spreads) on indexes, which can be profitable when the market is in sideways phase. In comparison to other strategies, index moves are less dramatic and far less likely to be influenced by the media.

CHAPTER 6: Advanced Trading Strategies

The good news is that with options, traders of all skill levels can learn how to trade the market. Options trading techniques typically utilize momentum metrics such as the Relative Strength Index (RSI) to warn them when market moves are overdone, either upside-down or downside-up, and are primed for reversal in the opposite direction. Also, traders tend to stay longer in a trade. It will make them better off to operate overnight as part of a swing trading plan, as acquired option positions have reduced downside danger. Option traders use a variety of options strategies which include buying and/or selling one or more options to take either directional or market-neutral views of the underlying asset market. These often usually use diagrams called option compensation or reward profiles to provide a quick understanding of whether the option plan would pay out with a variety of underlying market prices, including the one seen below, on the expiry date.

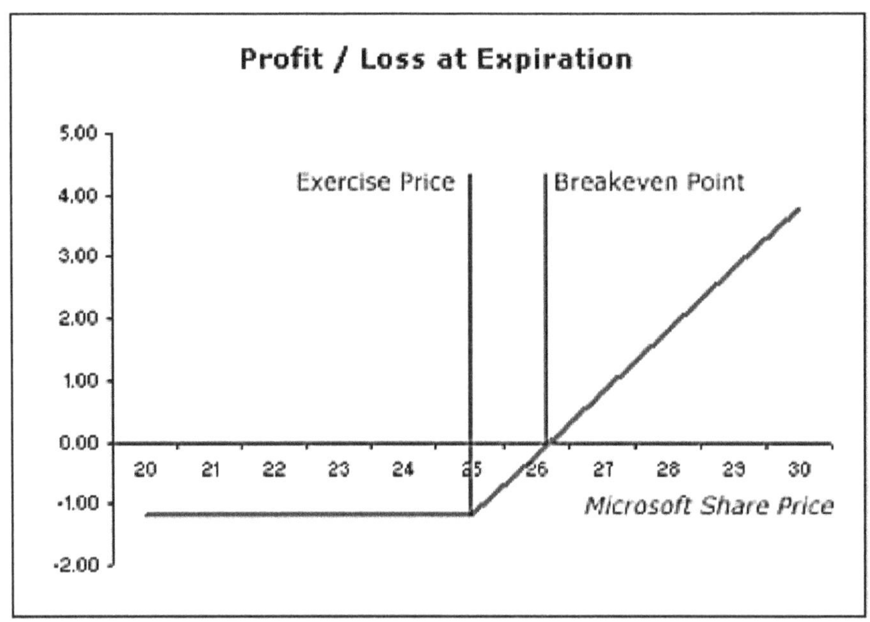

The blue line in that graph indicates how if the demand hits the breakeven stage, the option price begins making a profit at expiration. The position can also show a profit before expiry, however, if you can sell the option at a price higher than the purchase price. This is generally the goal when swinging trading the options. Fortunately, you can easily learn how to trade options to implement your market view for a directional trading strategy such as swing trading. The instructions below illustrate how to use a basic option strategy to swing trade in almost every financial asset sector where options are readily accessible, such as purchasing a call or put option.

Choose an asset

The first phase in swing trading with options is to pick an underlying commodity for trade that you have established as an incentive to sell. Swing traders would also track different equity markets in order to provide a better probability of having a successful trading setup. In picking an asset, search for equity price that is prone to a downturn as defined by a measure of momentum, such as the RSI. A specific measure is a range-bound oscillator that indicates an overbought position when its value is over 70 or oversold position when its value is below 30.

See when RSI moves above 70 and buy when it goes below 30

When you like any more accurate swing trading indications from the RSI, you should wait before you see something occurring called price-RSI variance, which implies that the market price rises briskly, such as reaching a new peak, but the RSI does not. That's an even stronger swing trading warning that an impending recession is coming to the market.

Select the right direction

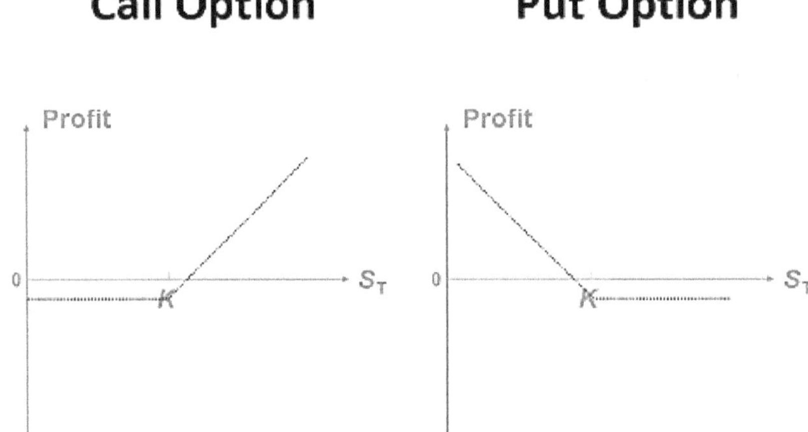

For example, once you've identified a market and used your preferred form of market analysis, whether technical and/or fundamental, to find a trading opportunity with a good risk / reward ratio of 2 or more to 1, then you might feel comfortable using call and/or put options to take a directional market view of the underlying asset. For example, if you think the market is going to rise, you would use a call option to go long in the market with limited downside risk and unlimited upside potential for the underlying market you want to trade.

Alternatively, if your view was that the market would fall, instead you would buy a put option, again with limited risk of downside and unlimited potential for upside. The payoff profiles below shown for long call and put options at expiry shows how your losses are limited to the premium paid if your directional view turns out to be wrong. In addition, potential profits on an option position are unlimited and begin to accumulate past the breakeven point where the gains on the position exceed the bonus paid.

Choose the strike price

An option's strike price aids in determining its price. Generally speaking, the more attractive an option's strike price is in relation to the prevailing market price for the underlying asset, the more it will cost. Also, the longer time frame a particular strike price option has until expiry, the more it will be expensive. When strike rates are higher than the prevalent sector, it is assumed that they are either "in the pocket" or ITM. An option with an ITM strike price also has "intrinsic value," corresponding to the difference between the prevailing market price (for the delivery date of the option) and the strike price. When the strike price of an option is right on the prevailing market, it is "at the money" or ATM, and when it is "out of the money," or OTM, at a level worse than the prevailing market. There is no inherent interest on both the ATM and OTM products. Many swing traders are trying to take advantage of reasonably short-term price fluctuations in a sector, and they are likely to choose an OTM opportunity as they expect ITM to go fairly fast thus enabling them to sell it back. This is because options also have time value as well as intrinsic value and as time progresses towards expiration, the time value declines increasingly. This encourages a swing trader to sell back any option that they bought when a respectable profit presents itself at the first opportunity.

Select expiration date

Choosing an expiry date would represent in part how long you believe it would take the underlying market to achieve your target price. Generally speaking, you'll want to choose a shorter-term option if you think the transfer would be fast or a longer-term option, especially if you think it could take more time. For a swing trader, you simply don't want to have an option that expires so early because it could end up being useless at expiration. At the other side, owing to the comparatively high cost, you do not want to purchase an option with an expiry date so long in the future.

Decide about the entry time

Timing of trading entries is usually done using technical analysis. Since swing traders deal both with patterns and with adjustments to such patterns, they first need to recognize, if any, the dominant pattern in the commodity they are looking at. Swing traders would look for a corrective pullback while trading with the trend to create a position in trend direction. If the pullback seems to be losing steam, as shown by an RSI level in over-bought or over-sold range, preferably indicating price deviation, they will believe the time to enter the market is ripe.

Execute the trade

When the time has come for the trade, it's time to proceed according to the trading schedule. For example, if the overall trend is higher, you could buy OTM call option, or an OTM put option if the market is downward. It's always crucial to note that the way you deal is just as critical as the point at which you sell, so make sure you pick the best broker as your business partner. Transaction costs can really add up over time, including handling spreads and fees, if you trade frequently as a swing trader.

Manage the position

You run the risk of failure after you have conducted a trade and have a choice, but because you bought an option, the liability would be restricted to the price you paid for it. You may always need to track the underlying demand to better handle the option trade. If you purchase an OTM share, you will decide to sell it until the underlying market hits the price of the strike and it is ATM. If the time value rises, that would also result in the option picking up extra prime. Competing with potential gains will be the time decay occurring for every full day an option approaches its expiry date. This suggests that at the earliest moment possible you'll want to sell back the option position to prevent making a deal centered on a perception that was directionally sound risk value due to premature deterioration over time. If the market still seems like your trade would finally pan out, but the short-term change you planned to capitalize on has failed to materialize will allow it more time to come to fruition.

It may be achieved by conducting a calendar spread or roll-out swap that includes selling back your own near-term option and purchasing a longer-term option at the same strike price. This prevents you from taking losses as their expiration approaches because of the sharply increasing time decay on near-money options.

Married Put

An investor purchases an asset in a married put strategy and at the same time purchases put options on an equal amount of securities. The buyer of the put option is entitled to sell the stock at the strike price, and the value of each contract is 100 shares. When keeping a stock, an investor can opt to use this strategy as a way to minimize their downside risk. For instance, suppose an investor buys 100 stock shares and simultaneously buys one put option. In the case of a significant shift in the market price, this approach could be beneficial to this investor since they are shielded from the downside. Around the same moment, if the asset rises in value, the investor will be able to participate in any possibility of upside. The main drawback to this approach is that the investor sacrifices the balance of the premium charged on the put option if the stock does not decrease in value.

Long Butterfly

Butterfly spread options are made up of 2 vertical spreads with a similar strike price. In other terms, an opening position where options (either calls or puts) are acquired (or sold) at 3 separate strike rates includes butterfly options. The method in which these options are produced renders the butterfly a position of both limited loses and limited benefits. It is possible to build the Long Butterfly spread option using either all call options or all put options. A Long Butterfly formed using call options would work like one generated using put options due to put-call parity. In other terms, it doesn't really matter if you make your Long Butterfly using calls or puts.

Short Iron Condor Strategy

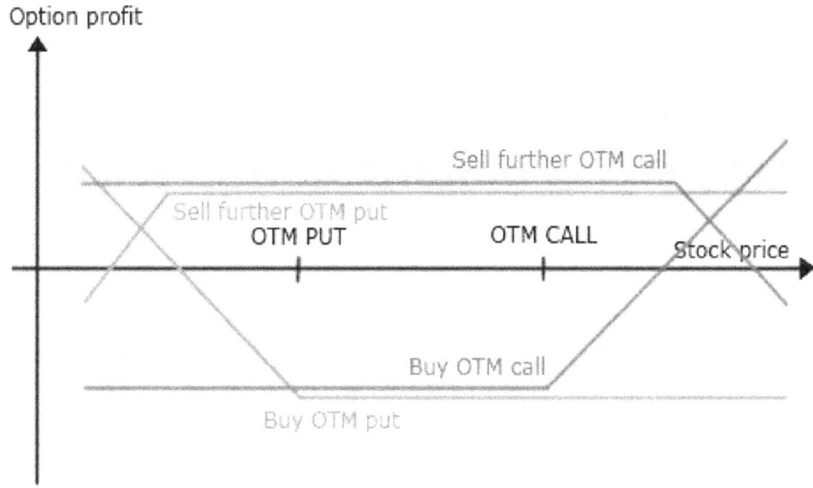

An advanced option trading technique that utilizes a mixture of two vertical spreads is the Iron Condor strategy. At strike prices that are greater than the current price of the underlying stock, a call spread is opened and a put spread is opened at strike prices which are lower than the current price. For volatile stocks, the Short Iron Condor technique is used. It is created by opening up a bullish out-of-the-money (OTM) call spread and a bearish out-of-the-money (OTM) put spread. You purchase an OTM call and you sell an extra OTM call. Then you purchase an OTM put then sell an OTM put, which is an extra OTM. This causes a scenario of debit spread, whereby when you open the position, you need to compensate the difference in premiums.

Long Iron Butterfly Options

The technique of the Iron Butterfly options is an advanced option strategy that uses 2 vertical spreads (1 call spread and 1 put spread) to build a position that is beneficial when you anticipate low volatility, or when you require great volatility but are unaware of the direction. The

Iron Butterfly is close to the strategies of the Butterfly and Iron Condor, as the name suggests. It has the same profile for profit and risk as the Butterfly, but uses a mix of option spreads similar to the Iron Condor. The most widely used variant of the Iron Butterfly is Long Iron Butterfly options. They are ideal for stocks that would not change significantly (low volatility).

Conclusion

You are not forced to buy or sell while trading options. You actually have the right to trade two kinds of stock options instead: puts and calls. Participants in new options are enthusiastic about the advantages participants earn and make errors. There are certain errors that you must avoid during options trading like starting too big, using only one strategy, setting an illogical expiration date, purchasing out-of-the-money options and increasing the trades for making up losses. New option traders end up exacerbating their risk. Close failed trades instead of attempting to solve problems that have already damaged you and your money. When you understand when to close trades, you move a step closer to transitioning from a novice to a good option investor. A perfect way is to take a time-out and rest your minds from trading. Taking a break is going to really ideally place things in order. Understand, you're not going to lose much in a couple of hours, which is time to calm off. After all, a number of wonderful prospects are always waiting for you, just losing one or two carry no meanings and shall have no impact on your performance. It's better to live with the heat of passion than to risk all the capital. You just have to learn start trading with a cold head and enjoy your trades in the options market.

www.ingramcontent.com/pod-product-compliance
Lightning Source LLC
Chambersburg PA
CBHW080502030726
47592CB00011B/3222